William Bolcom

T0083948

Nine New Bagatelles

Piano Solo

ISBN 1-423-40840-3

BOLCOM MUSIC

EDWARD B.
MARKS MUSIC
COMPANY

EXCLUSIVELY DISTRIBUTED BY

HAL•LEONARD®
CORPORATION

7777 W. BLUEMOUND RD. P.O. BOX 13819 MILWAUKEE, WI 53213

Visit Hal Leonard Online at
www.halleonard.com

NOTES

I — Tell a story.

II — The gesture is more important than the notes.

III — To be played with the greatest freedom.

IV — Play without putting your bodily weight in the keys. (The reference is to a famous English tale of a young bride playing hide-and-seek from her elderly new husband, Lord Livell; hiding in a trunk, she succeeds all too well and is only discovered decades later, a skeleton in a bridal dress.) In this Bagatelle there are only two accents and two tenutos.

V — Play expressively and lyrically, in strong contrast to IV. As with I, tell a story—this time a whole life in miniature.

VI — Play as mechanically as possible.

VII — This piece should be perceived as if through a fog; it is about the failure of memory.

VIII — A continuous wedge of sound despite the pauses.

IX — Play as dramatically as possible; if the minor-ninth RH chords in mm. 21 to 23 are too big a handspan for the player, change to:

—WB

ACCIDENTALS

N.B. Accidentals obtain throughout a beamed group. Unbeamed notes within a measure continue the same accidental until interrupted by another note or rest. (Additional courtesy accidentals are given to ensure clarity.) In music with key signatures, traditional rules apply.

William Bolcom

Nine New Bagatelles

for piano

I.	(. . . "and then what happened?")
II.	(. . . what happened)
III.	(. . . a bird comments—to another bird?)
IV.	(. . . Lord Lovell's trunk)
V.	(. . . a little story)
VI.	(. . . take no prisoners)
VII.	(. . . valse oubliable)
VIII.	(. . .benediction)
IX.	(. . . pavane for the dead / hope's feathers)

*Commissioned by the "Friends of Today's Music" program
of the Music Teacher's Association of California*

NINE NEW BAGATELLES
for piano

WILLIAM BOLCOM

(. . . "and then what happened?")

6

(. . . what happened)

III. **Bold**   **Slower, plaintive**   **Tempo I**

(. . . a bird comments—to another bird?)

IV. **Ghostly** ($\bullet$ = 69), *like a phantom harpsichord*

(. . . Lord Lovell's trunk)

V. **Andante** ♩ = c. 60

(. . . a little story)

VI. **Very even** (♩ = 138)

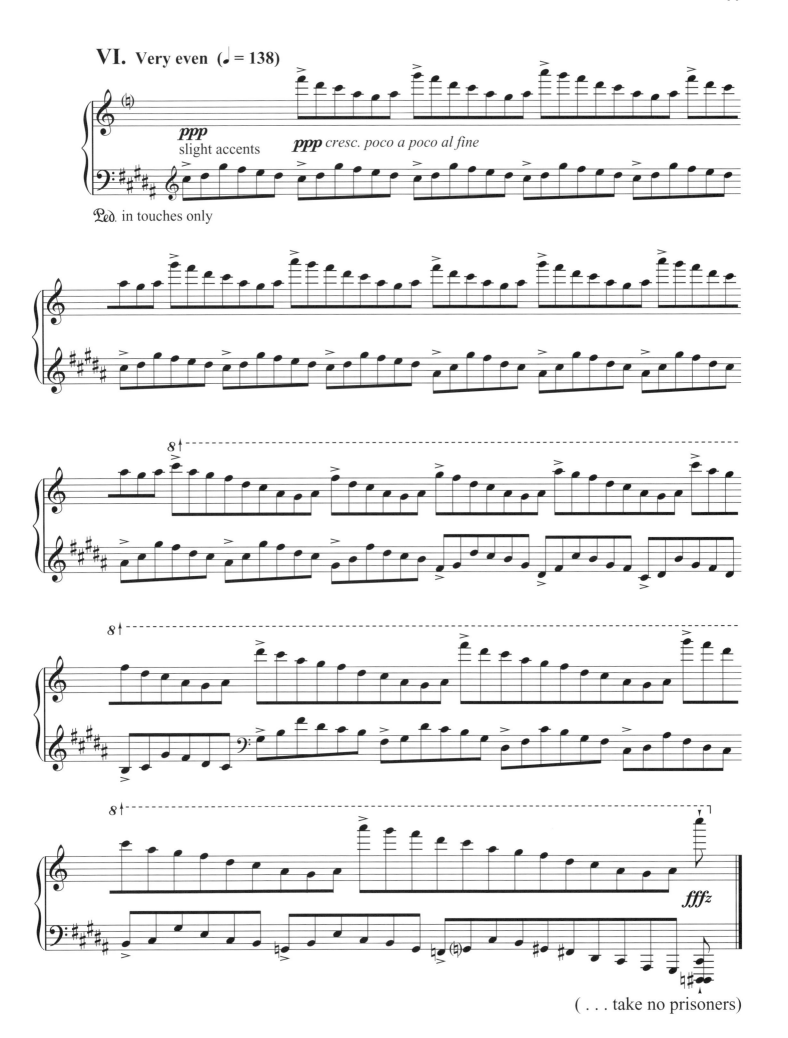

ppp
slight accents

ppp *cresc. poco a poco al fine*

Ped. in touches only

fff z

(. . . take no prisoners)

VII. With a swing (♩. = 50, *not strict*)

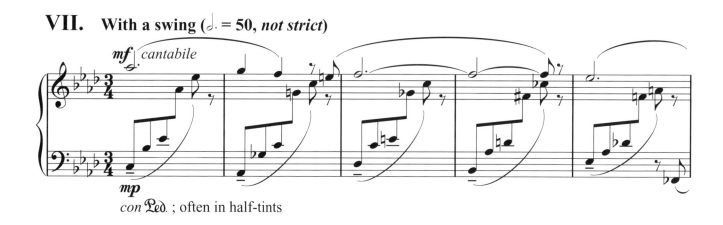

con 𝖯𝖾𝖽. ; often in half-tints

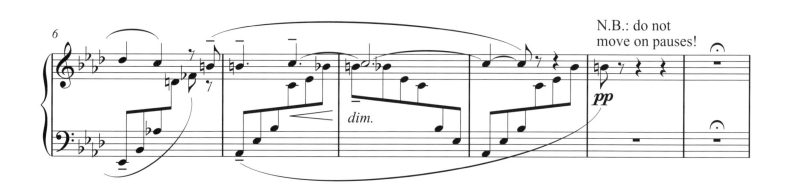

N.B.: do not
move on pauses!

poch. rit. a tempo
con calore

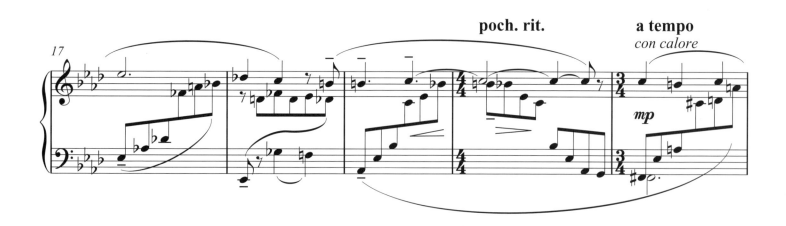

Slower

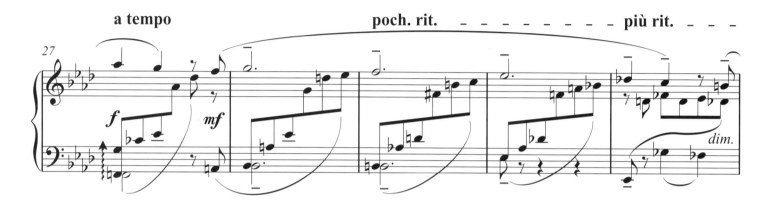

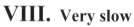

(. . . valse oubliable)

VIII. **Very slow**

(. . . benediction)

IX. Alla marcia funebre (♩ = 60)

*see NOTES, p. 2

(. . . pavane for the dead / hope's feathers)